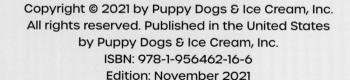

To see more of our books, visit us at:
www.PuppyDogsAndIceCream.com

LEARN

FUN FACTS

SIZE

WEIGHT

LOCATION

AGES 3-10

THE FANTASTIC WORLD OF
Fish

Dr. Melanie Stiassny of the
American Museum of Natural History

FUN FACTS
About Our
Marine Friends

About the Author

My name is Melanie Stiassny, and I am an **ichthyologist** – which means that I am someone who studies fish. I work at the **American Museum of Natural History** and my title is **Curator of Fishes**. It is a great job and I get to travel all around the world learning about the animals I love, and sometimes I even discover and get to name new species.

Our planet is often called The Blue Planet, because over 70% of its surface is covered in water and living in all that water are lots and lots of fish. In fact, **there are more species of fish than there are mammals, birds, reptiles, and amphibians all added together!**

Fish live just about anywhere there is water – from the highest mountain streams to the deepest depths of the oceans. They come in almost every imaginable shape, size, and color and all are beautifully adapted to thrive in the places where they live.

I have been studying fish all my career and yet still **I learn something new about them every day**. I very much hope that you will enjoy this book and that it will teach you something new about some of these wonderful animals that we share our planet with - perhaps it will even make you to want to learn more about them.

Dr. Melanie Stiassny
Curator of Fishes
American Museum of Natural History

Whale Shark

Rhincodon typus

FUN FACTS

Whale sharks are the largest fish in the world. The name "whale shark" refers to the fish's size, being as large as some species of whales.

Whale sharks have huge, flattened heads

They are grayish blue with lots of white spots

Their large, oval mouth is as wide as their body

These "gentle giants" are no threat to humans and will allow divers to swim close to them

Where do they live?
Circumglobal in all tropical and warm temperate waters

How big are they?
Largest ever recorded:
75,000 lbs = a fire truck
56 feet = a semi truck

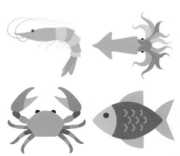

What do they eat?
Small fish, crustaceans, and squids

Pacific Sailfish

Istiophorus platypterus

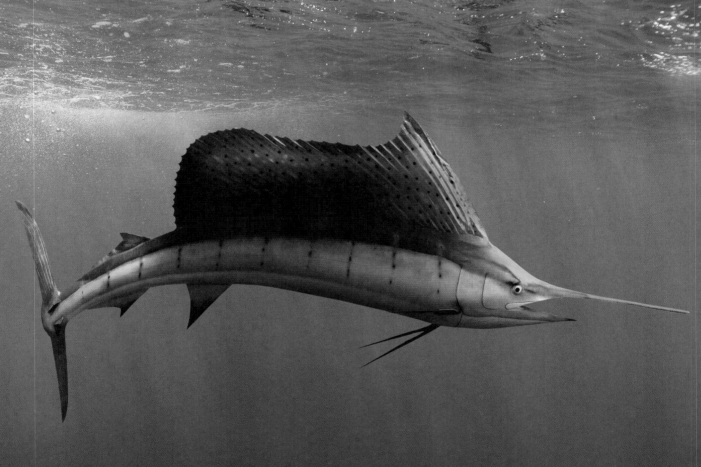

FUN FACTS

Pacific sailfish can swim nearly 70 mph, making them the fastest fish in the world.

When swimming fast, the dorsal fin is folded down tight against its body as it speeds through the water like a torpedo

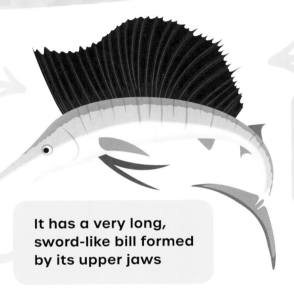

This fish gets its name from its huge dorsal fin which resembles the sail of a boat

It has a very long, sword-like bill formed by its upper jaws

Where do they live?
Indo-Pacific in tropical and warm temperate waters

How big are they?
Largest ever recorded:
220 lbs = a refrigerator
11.5 feet long = 2 men

What do they eat?
Mainly fish but also crustaceans and squids

Atlantic Blue Marlin

Makaira nigricans

FUN FACTS

It uses its "bill" to slash and stun prey, making them easier to catch. Females are up to four times bigger than males.

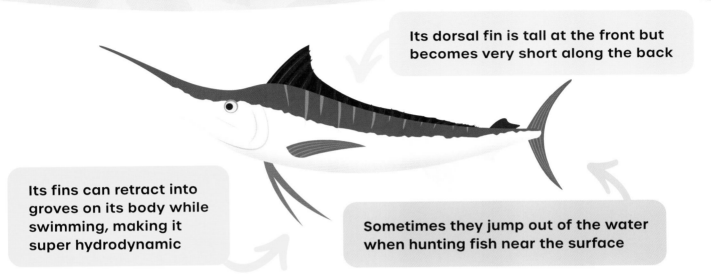

Its dorsal fin is tall at the front but becomes very short along the back

Its fins can retract into groves on its body while swimming, making it super hydrodynamic

Sometimes they jump out of the water when hunting fish near the surface

Where do they live?
Tropical and temperate waters of the Atlantic Ocean

How big are they?
Largest ever recorded:
1,400 lbs = sailboat
16.4 feet = a car

What do they eat?
Mainly fish but also octopus and squids

Giant Manta Ray

Mobula birostris

FUN FACTS

Giant manta ray don't lay eggs but instead give birth to one or two "pups" which are about 4 feet wide when born.

It has two flaps on the sides of its face to help direct water and plankton into its mouth

It swims by slowly flapping its huge wing-like fins

They have a long, whip-like tail with no stinger

It is black with white patches on top and white underneath

Where do they live?
Circumglobal in tropical and subtropical waters

How big are they?
Largest ever recorded:
6,600 lbs = 2 cars
30 foot wingspan = a school bus

What do they eat?
Plankton and small fish

Clown Anemonefish

Amphiprion ocellaris

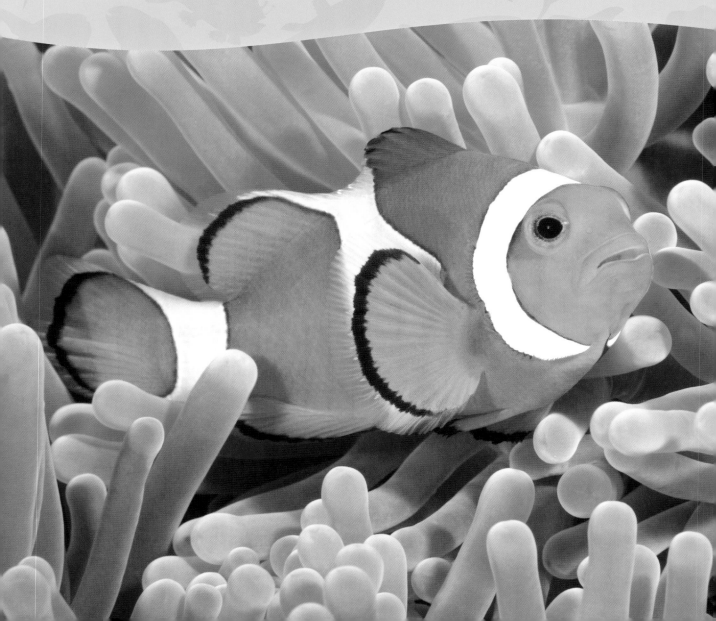

FUN FACTS

Clown anemonefish are immune to the sting of sea anemones, and use this to its advantage by taking shelter inside.

They are bright orange with three white stripes

These fish can live between 3-10 years

They live in family groups in the same anemone, sometimes for generations

Where do they live?
Coral reefs in the Indo-Pacific ocean

How big are they?
Largest ever recorded:
9 oz = a hamster
4.5 inches = a soda can

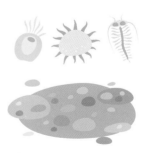

What do they eat?
Plankton and algae

Hairy Frogfish

Antennarius striatus

FUN FACTS

Hairy frogfish have a dorsal fin modified into a worm-shaped "lure" that hangs over its mouth and wiggles to attract prey.

They stay completely still as they use their lure to bring prey close to their mouth

They can swallow prey almost as large as themselves

Its skin is covered with thin spines that look like strands of algae for camouflage

It uses its limb-like fins to walk along the sea floor

Where do they live?
Atlantic and Indo-Pacific Oceans around inshore reefs

How big are they?
Largest ever recorded:
1.2 oz = a light-bulb
10 inches long = an envelope

What do they eat?
Crustaceans, fish, and even other frogfish

Indian Ocean Coelacanth

Latimeria chalumnae

FUN FACTS

They were thought to have become extinct about 66 million years ago, but in 1938 one was discovered alive off the coast of South Africa.

Irregular, white spots are scattered all over its body

They are a dark, metallic blue in color with thick, bony scales

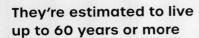

They're estimated to live up to 60 years or more

They give birth to live young

Where do they live?
Western Indian Ocean

How big are they?
Largest ever recorded:
210 lbs = a refrigerator
6.5 feet long = a bed

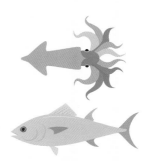

What do they eat?
Large fish and squids

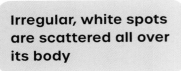

Greenland Shark

Somniosus microcephalus

FUN FACTS

Greenland sharks don't reach maturity until they are about 150 years old, and the oldest known Greenland shark was 392 years old.

Thickset and so slow moving, these sharks are sometimes called sleeper sharks

They prefer to live in waters that are between 30-50° F

Colors range from a creamy-gray to brownish black

Where do they live?
Deep, cold waters of the Northern Atlantic and Arctic Ocean

How big are they?
Largest ever recorded:
1700 lbs = a horse
18 feet long = a giraffe

What do they eat?
Eats just about anything, but mainly large fish

Leafy Sea Dragon

Phycodurus eques

FUN FACTS

Female sea dragons lay their eggs on the tails of males. The males carry the eggs for about a month before they hatch into tiny baby sea-dragons.

Their skin color helps them blend in with seaweeds and kelp

They have spines mixed in with the leaf-like lobes for defense

They use a straw-like mouth to slurp up food

Where do they live?
South Australian coastal waters around rocky kelp-covered reefs

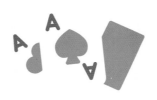

How big are they?
Largest ever recorded:
3.5 oz = a deck of cards
17 inches = a bowling pin

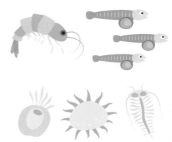

What do they eat?
Tiny crustaceans, fish larvae, and other plankton

Ocean Sunfish

Mola mola

FUN FACTS

Ocean sunfish are the heaviest of all bony fish. A single female sunfish was found to contain 300 million eggs.

They have a beak-like structure for a mouth

The sunfish doesn't have a tail, instead it has what's called a clavus

Often found floating on its side at the ocean surface, sun-bathing

They have long dorsal and belly fins

Where do they live?
Circumglobal, in tropical and temperate waters

How big are they?
Largest ever recorded:
5000 lbs = an elephant
14 feet = a small car

What do they eat?
Jellyfish, crustaceans, mollusks, brittle stars, and fish

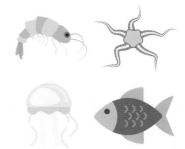

Beluga Sturgeon

Huso huso

FUN FACTS

They rival the great white shark for the world's largest predatory fish. Its eggs are the most expensive in the world and are called beluga caviar.

Because of years of over-fishing this fish is critically endangered

They have rows of strong, bony plates called scutes instead of scales like other fish

Four long barbels hang down in front of its wide mouth and help it locate food

They can live up to 50 years in the wild and 100 years in captivity

Where do they live?
Caspian, Black, and Azov Seas

How big are they?
Largest ever recorded:
3,000 lbs = a car
24 feet long = a bus

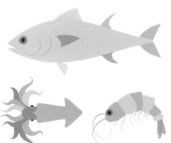

What do they eat?
Mostly fish, crustaceans, and squids

Atlantic Bluefin Tuna

Thunnus thynnus

FUN FACTS

Atlantic bluefin tuna are the largest of the tuna species. It hunts by sight and is thought to have the sharpest vision of all bony fish.

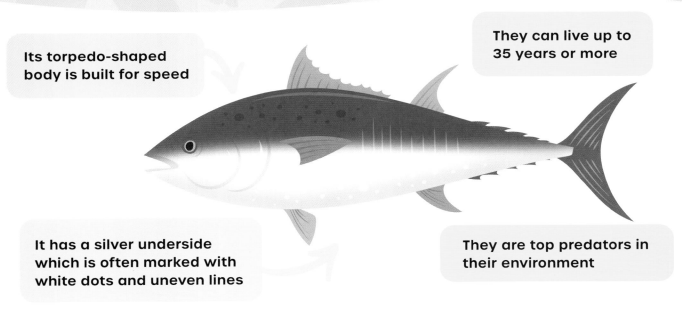

Its torpedo-shaped body is built for speed

They can live up to 35 years or more

It has a silver underside which is often marked with white dots and uneven lines

They are top predators in their environment

Where do they live?
Atlantic Ocean

How big are they?
Largest ever recorded:
1,500 lbs = a bull
15 feet = a car

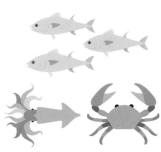

What do they eat?
Small schooling fish, squids, and crabs

Mandarinfish

Synchiropus splendidus

FUN FACTS

Mandarinfish are one of the most colorful fish. They have no scales and are able to secrete a poisonous mucous as a defense.

Males have a longer, pointed dorsal fin while females have round ones

When looking for a mate they perform a colorful courtship dance

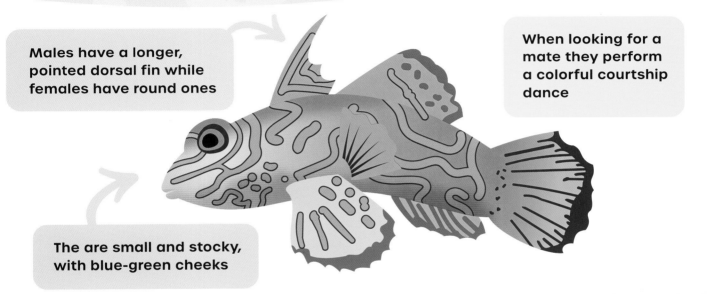

The are small and stocky, with blue-green cheeks

Where do they live?
Western Pacific Ocean in lagoons and inshore reefs

How big are they?
Largest ever recorded:
5 oz = a baseball
3 inches long = a credit card

What do they eat?
Small snails, worms, fish eggs, and plankton

Long-spined Porcupinefish

Diodon holocanthus

FUN FACTS

When threatened they can inflate into a spiky ball by taking water into their body. They can expand to about three times their normal size.

When not inflated, their spines lay flat against their sleek body

It may look like a pufferfish but, while closely related, they are not the same

When inflated, their spines stick out in every direction

Where do they live?
Circumtropical, in reefs and inshore shallows

How big are they?
Largest ever recorded:
1 lbs = a soccer ball
20 inches = 2 envelopes

What do they eat?
Mollusks, sea urchins, and crabs

Atlantic Herring

Clupea harengus

FUN FACTS

The Atlantic herring are one of the most abundant fish species in the world. Sometimes millions gather covering almost a cubic mile of ocean.

It is a slim, elongate fish with a single, small dorsal fin

They travel together in large groups for defense against predators

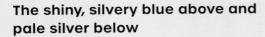

The shiny, silvery blue above and pale silver below

They are one of the world's most important fish since they feed so many other animals

Where do they live?
Northern Pacific and Atlantic Oceans, and Baltic Sea

=

How big are they?
Largest ever recorded:
2.4 lbs = bottle of water
18 inches long = a bowling pin

What do they eat?
Plankton, krill, and small fish

Dolphin Fish

Coryphaena hippurus

FUN FACTS

Also known as mahi-mahi, in Hawaiian it means "strong-strong". They are difficult to catch on fishing lines because of their strength.

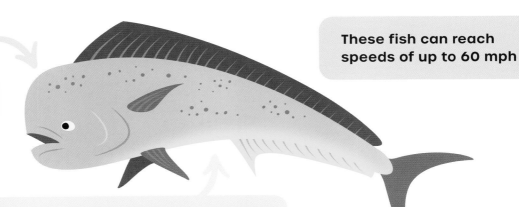

These fish can reach speeds of up to 60 mph

Males have very large, prominent foreheads

While a dazzling, iridescent bluish-green and yellow in the water, they quickly lose their bright colors when taken out of it

Where do they live?
Circumglobal in tropical and subtropical waters

How big are they?
Largest ever recorded:
88 lbs = a very large dog
7 feet long = a Christmas tree

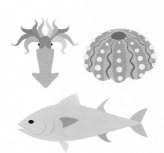

What do they eat?
Small fish, squid, and crustaceans

Red Sea
Steephead Parrotfish
Chlorurus gibbus

FUN FACTS

They have fused beak-like teeth which they use to crush coral and eat the algae growing on it. Each adult can crunch up tons of coral a year.

Their fused teeth form an almost bird-like beak

By eating the algae, these fish help maintain the health of the coral reef

Parrotfish have different colors based on their age and gender

Where do they live?
The Red Sea

How big are they?
Largest ever recorded:
8.8 lbs = 9 bunches of bananas
2.3 feet long = a small baseball bat

What do they eat?
Algae grazed from coral

Giant Guitarfish

Rhynchobatus djiddensis

FUN FACTS

Guitarfish are bottom feeders and can bury themselves in sand. When prey approach they suddenly emerge from the sand and attack.

Its eyes are on top of its head so it can see while buried

It looks like a blend between a skate and a shark

Their coloration helps them blend in with the sand

It has a flattened guitar-shaped body

Where do they live?
Western Indian Ocean and Red Sea

How big are they?
Largest ever recorded:
500 lbs = a pig
10 feet long = basketball hoop

What do they eat?
Clams, crabs, lobsters, and small fish

Photograph Credits and Copyrights.

CLAIM YOUR FREE GIFT!

Visit

PDICBooks.com/Gift

Thank you for purchasing
The Fantastic World of Fish,
and welcome to the Puppy Dogs & Ice Cream family.

We're certain you're going to love
the little gift we've prepared for you
at the website above.